Handwriting Practice Paper

100 Handwriting Practice Pages with Block Alphabet Tracing Chart included:

+

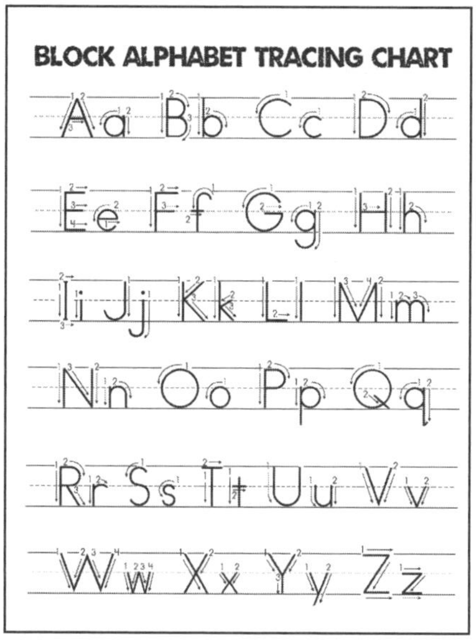

BONUS Alphabet Chart on the Back Cover too!

TEACHER TIP: for durability, cut out and laminate the alphabet tracing chart page. After laminated, use a dry erase marker to practice tracing according to the arrows, wipe away, and repeat.

My name is

BLOCK ALPHABET TRACING CHART

Aa Bb Cc Dd
Ee Ff Gg Hh
Ii Jj Kk Ll Mm
Nn Oo Pp Qq
Rr Ss Tt Uu Vv
Ww Xx Yy Zz